SUCH IS
THE REAL NATURE
OF HORSES

Horses have hooves t[...]
snow, and hair to prote[...]
They eat grass and dri[...]
tails and gallop. Cerer[...]
ings are of no use to th[...]
rub their necks togeth[...]
round and kick up thei[...]
the real nature of hors[...]

T[